NAPOLEON & PARIS

JEAN-FRANÇOIS LOZIER

© **Canadian Museum of History 2016**

All rights reserved. No part of this book may be reproduced or transmitted in any form or by any means, electronic or mechanical, including photocopying, recording or any retrieval system, without the prior written permission of the Canadian Museum of History. Every effort has been made to obtain permission for all copyright-protected work presented in this publication. If you have copyright-protected work in this publication and have not given permission, or to enquire about reproducing any section of this publication, please contact permissions@historymuseum.ca.

Library and Archives Canada
Cataloguing in Publication

Lozier, Jean-François, author
Napoleon and Paris /
Jean-François Lozier.

(Souvenir catalogue series, ISSN 2291-6385; 16)
Issued also in French under title: Napoléon et Paris.
ISBN 978-0-660-03698-4 (paperback)

Cat. no.: NM23-5/16-2016E

1. Napoleon I, Emperor of the French, 1769-1821 – Homes and haunts – France – Paris – Exhibitions.
2. Paris (France) – History – 1799-1815 – Exhibitions.
I. Canadian Museum of History, issuing body.
II. Title.
III. Series: Souvenir catalogue series; 16.

DC203.9.L69 2016
944.05092
C2016-902909-3

Published by the
Canadian Museum of History
100 Laurier Street
Gatineau, QC K1A 0M8
historymuseum.ca

Printed and bound in Canada.

This work is a souvenir of the exhibition **Napoleon and Paris**, which was produced by the Musée Carnavalet – Histoire de Paris, Paris Musées and the Canadian Museum of History.

Souvenir Catalogue series, 16

ISSN 2291-6385

TABLE OF CONTENTS

5   Foreword

9   Introduction

13   A Chronicle of Napoleon and Paris

51   The Administration of the City

63   The Court at the Tuileries

77   The City of His Dreams

95   The Legend in Paris

FOREWORD

Napoleon and Paris…. The man and the city — their moments of greatness and their less glorious aspects — have left an imprint on the collective imagination. The story of this formidable duo is told here concisely in words and pictures.

A seasoned military leader, Napoleon also proved to be a visionary and an outstanding administrator as First Consul and then Emperor. He strove to give the city he loved the prestige and infrastructure that would turn it into a "New Rome," hoping to make it the capital of Europe. Worn out and bruised by the French Revolution, Paris was very receptive to the unifying message of its new leader, as well as to his wish to maintain law and order, and restore the pomp and pageantry of the Ancien Régime.

Over a period of about fifteen years, Bonaparte reorganized his capital and transformed its appearance by endowing the city with many utilitarian structures and magnificent buildings. Fully aware of the power of images and symbols, he adorned it with jewels and gave it a new look, inspired by an idealized and updated antiquity. Years after Napoleon's death on St. Helena, Paris received his remains with great pomp, and it sang the praises of its emperor long after.

The *Napoleon and Paris* souvenir catalogue is a companion to the exhibition produced by the Musée Carnavalet – Histoire de Paris and adapted by the Canadian Museum of History, with the support of Paris Musées. By presenting exhibitions of international calibre, the Museum is pursuing its mission to safeguard our collective memory and to present to Canadians events and subjects that transcend time and place. Exhibitions such as this help us to better understand the world we have inherited and the lasting influence of the past on our identity today.

This souvenir catalogue presents the exhibition's major themes. In it, readers will discover many period illustrations and precious objects — clothing, furniture, paintings, prints and models — that reveal the close ties that bound Napoleon Bonaparte to the City of Light and vibrantly bring to life important moments of his years in Paris.

Jean-Marc Blais
Director General
Canadian Museum of History

"I sometimes dreamt of making Paris the true capital of Europe. At times, I wanted it to become … something fabulous, colossal, something the world had never seen before …"

— *Napoleon*

Portrait of Napoleon I

1809
Robert Lefèvre
Oil on canvas

This portrait, commissioned for Paris's city hall, depicts the Emperor as a military leader. Standing in front of his work table, he wears his best-known uniform, that of a colonel in the *chasseurs à cheval* of the Imperial Guard, a light cavalry unit. For everyday wear, the Emperor preferred this plain uniform, rather than an ornate one.

INTRODUCTION

Napoleon Bonaparte's remarkable life is inextricably linked to Paris. A man of war, Napoleon made Paris the capital of an empire. A man of ambition, he revived its vibrant court life.

A man of vision, he reshaped the city and endowed it with enduring institutions. Two centuries after the end of the First Empire, this exhibition and catalogue invite you to discover the complex relationship that has forever linked Napoleon and Paris.

We begin with a chronicle highlighting fourteen key moments in the relationship between the man and the city. During his fifteen years in power, Napoleon spent more time on battlefields than in his capital. Still, from his rise to his fall, Paris was the main stage on which the Napoleonic epic unfolded. It was where Napoleon's government was transformed into a monarchy, and where its leader chose to be crowned emperor. The fate of the imperial regime was also decided in Paris, when Napoleon abdicated there for the second and last time, after his defeat at Waterloo.

From moments, we then turn our attention to themes: the administration of the capital, court life, construction projects and the Napoleonic legend.

Napoleon did his best to gain exclusive control of Paris and its 650,000 or so inhabitants. Having assumed power following a decade of political instability, he knew that it was in Paris that regimes were made and unmade. He reorganized the city's administration, entrusting it to public servants who reported directly to him. To oversee the general population and its needs, he reformed old institutions and established new ones. He also placed public spaces under heavy surveillance.

Napoleon put some distance between himself and his subjects. In the days of the Consulate and the Empire, he revived the pageantry of the fallen monarchy. He chose to move into the Tuileries, a former royal palace that had been the last official residence of Louis XVI. Little by little, court life re-emerged there. A host of dignitaries gravitated around the imperial family.

This luxurious setting satisfied the Emperor's taste for comfort and, above all, his desire for order and his politics of splendour. New official orders revived production in the Parisian luxury-goods industry. The exhibition provides a glimpse into the work of some of the artists and artisans who were active in the capital at the time: the painter Boilly; the Jacob family, cabinetmakers;

the goldsmith Biennais; the locksmith Desouches; the hatmaker Poupard; and Percier and Fontaine, the era's leading team of architects.

Paris looked more or less the same as it had under Louis XVI, and Napoleon wanted to make it stand out. He decided to fill it with monuments largely inspired by those of antiquity, but he also innovated by attaching as much importance to utilitarian facilities as to prestigious buildings. Bridges, quays, canals and fountains were built, and slaughterhouses, as well as outdoor and covered markets, appeared throughout the city. The new Napoleonic Paris was as much a city of amenities as a city of monuments.

The fall of the Empire put an end to many projects, but Napoleon was not forgotten. He remained very present in the collective memory. His tragic fate — his exile and death on St. Helena — added to his legend. Others completed some of the monuments he had begun. Trying to take advantage of its former adversary's prestige, the restored monarchy had his remains transferred to Paris and laid to rest at Les Invalides.

With the advent of Napoleon III and the Second Empire, even as the city underwent significant transformations, the legend reached its greatest heights. Although much has changed since the days of Napoleon I, the Parisian landscape continues to bear his mark to this day.

Napoleon's Throne

**Around 1805–1809
François-Honoré-Georges
Jacob-Desmalter and
Georges Jacob**

This armchair is depicted in the background of the portrait of Napoleon (page 8). Like much of the Emperor's furniture, it came from the workshop of the most famous Parisian cabinetmakers of the time.

A CHRONICLE OF NAPOLEON AND PARIS

"A great capital is the homeland of a nation's elite … it is the centre of opinion, the repository of everything."

— *Napoleon*

1784–1799
Bonaparte in Paris

Napoleone Buonaparte was born far from Paris, in Ajaccio, Corsica, on August 15, 1769. The island, to whose gentry his family belonged, had recently been conquered by France. And thus it was to France that the young Napoleon, as he would become known, went to study.

He began his military training in Brienne and completed it in Paris, at the École royale militaire, in 1784-1785. He graduated with the rank of second lieutenant in the artillery.

Bonaparte was not in Paris when the French Revolution broke out. In June 1789, representatives of the French people challenged royal absolutism and formed a National Assembly. The following month, revolutionary mobs took the Bastille, a prison and symbol of authority.

While passing through the capital three years later, however, Napoleon witnessed the two dramatic days of the Revolution: the occupation of the Tuileries royal palace, in June, and the fall of the monarchy, in August. The revolutionary excesses that he witnessed made him loathe mass movements and be wary of them. Back in Paris, and newly promoted to the rank of general, on October 5, 1795 (13 Vendémiaire, Year IV in the revolutionary calendar), he did not hesitate to use cannons against royalist insurgents who

Bust of Napoleon Bonaparte

1798
Charles-Louis Corbet
Plaster

were marching on the National Convention — the assembly that governed the French Republic — resulting in 300 deaths.

Around that time, Bonaparte — who had been nicknamed General Vendémiaire — fell madly in love with an attractive widow born in Martinique, Marie Josèphe Rose Tascher de La Pagerie, whose husband, Alexandre de Beauharnais, had been executed two years earlier. Since she was destitute and had two young children to support, her survival instinct led her to marry General Bonaparte on March 9, 1796. Although she had always used the name Rose, she adopted the name Josephine to please her new husband.

The Revolutionary Wars took Bonaparte away from the capital once again. From March 1796 to December 1797, he was the general in charge of the French forces in Italy, and from May 1798 to October 1799, he led the French forces in Egypt. As Bonaparte's star rose, that of the Directory — the regime that replaced the Convention — faded.

Josephine de Beauharnais

1799
Andrea Appiani
Oil on canvas

Napoleon and the Council of Five Hundred

1800
Isidore-Stanislas Helman, after Charles Monnet
Etching and engraving

1799
The *Coup d'État* of 18 Brumaire

Viewed by many as the saviour of the French Republic, upon his return from Egypt, Napoleon Bonaparte agreed to provide the military force needed for a plot aimed at overthrowing the Directory.

On November 9, 1799 (18 Brumaire, Year VIII in the revolutionary calendar), Bonaparte and his two co-conspirators, Emmanuel-Joseph Sieyès and Pierre Roger Ducos, both of whom had been Directors up to that point, put their plan into action. The next day, they had the Council of Five Hundred transferred to the Château de Saint-Cloud and then tried to impose a revision of the Constitution, but most of the members of that legislative assembly opposed them. There was a violent scene. Bonaparte had to be protected by his grenadiers, as he was taken to task by members clamouring, "Down with the dictator, outlaw!" His brother Lucien, president of the Council, attempted to maintain order. The Council of Five Hundred was dispersed.

On the third day, November 11, a few elected officials were located to pass a law that replaced the Directory with three provisional consuls: Bonaparte, Sieyès and Roger Ducos. The consuls were assigned the task of drafting a new constitution.

The *coup d'état* was not contested by the people. Most Parisians, like the majority of the population of France, were in favour of it.

1799
The Consulate

On December 13, a new constitution was adopted. It was submitted to the French people for approval, accompanied by a proclamation by the consuls: "Citizens, the Revolution is anchored on the principles that gave birth to it; it is over." The Directory was supplanted by a new regime, the Consulate.

Sieyès and Roger Ducos were cast aside as three permanent consuls were installed: Jean-Jacques Régis de Cambacérès, Charles-François Lebrun and Bonaparte. The latter was named First Consul. In theory, he shared power with the other two. However, as head of the executive, he had the last word, and his colleagues could not oppose him.

He had the power to propose legislation and make appointments to the principal positions in the public service, in addition to significant power with regard to diplomatic and military affairs.

Bonaparte's military victory against the Austrians at Marengo, Italy, on June 14, 1800, gave new legitimacy to the *coup d'état*. The First Consul was on the road to absolute power.

First Consul Bonaparte's Portfolio

1799–1804
Attributed to Martin-Guillaume Biennais
Leather

Explosion of an Infernal Machine

Around 1800–1801
Coloured etching

1800
An Assassination Attempt on Rue Saint-Nicaise

In both royalist and republican circles, there were still opponents to the Consulate. The police had trouble keeping an eye on the most radical ones who were plotting against the regime.

Chouan conspirators — royalists from Brittany — decided to kill First Consul Bonaparte. They designed an "infernal machine" composed of cases of grapeshot and barrels of gunpowder. This bomb, which was supposed to explode as Napoleon passed by, was placed on a cart set up on Rue Saint-Nicaise, north of the Tuileries Palace.

On the evening of December 24, 1800, Napoleon went to the opera with Josephine. The bomb went off just after their carriage passed. Miraculously, Bonaparte emerged unscathed, but 22 people were killed and around 100 were wounded in the assassination attempt, which destroyed about 50 houses.

1801–1802
The Concordat and Peace

Bonaparte's popularity was at its height during the Consulate because he brought peace to a country that had been torn apart by the Revolution.

Revolutionary France was an enemy of Catholicism, which, until then, had been the dominant religion in the country. Shortly after the *coup d'état*, Bonaparte sought to settle this issue, which greatly undermined national unity. On July 15, 1801, he signed a treaty — the Concordat — with the Holy See. The pope recognized the Republic and accepted its legislation related to civil status, marriage and divorce.

Bonaparte also ushered in peace beyond France's borders by signing treaties with major powers that had opposed revolutionary France. On February 9, 1801, the Peace of Lunéville put an end to the lengthy conflict with the House of Austria. That of Amiens, signed on March 25, 1802, sealed the peace with Great Britain. But war soon resumed with Britain a year later, and with Austria three years after that.

In 1802, Bonaparte became First Consul for life.

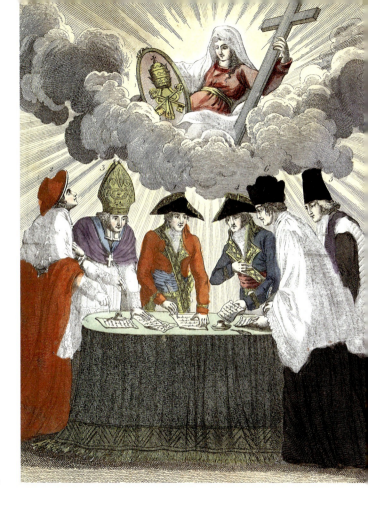

The Signing of the Concordat

1801
Coloured etching

Georges Cadoudal Being Arrested

1804
Coloured etching

1804
The Cadoudal Conspiracy and the Execution of the Duke of Enghien

Another conspiracy tainted the First Consul's rise to power. Georges Cadoudal, the leader of the royalists who had been opposing the Republic for more than a decade, plotted to kill or capture Bonaparte.

In January 1804, the police learned that Cadoudal and his men were in Paris, and posted notices to encourage their denunciation. That led to a wave of violent arrests. On March 9, 1804, when the police found Cadoudal, a wild chase followed through the streets of Paris, on horseback and on foot. Cadoudal killed two of the officers who sought to arrest him. He was tried, condemned to death and guillotined with eleven of his accomplices.

Apprehended for having supported Cadoudal's plan, General Pichegru was found strangled with his cravat in his cell. Bonaparte's enemies maintained loudly and strongly that the apparent suicide was an assassination.

Cadoudal's trial revealed that the conspirators were awaiting the arrival of a member of the royal family. Suspicion fell upon the Duke of Enghien, and Napoleon had him arrested. On March 15, 1804, a cavalry squadron seized the young duke past the border in Germany and took him to Paris. Summarily tried, he was condemned by a military commission and executed. The act sparked waves of indignation toward the First Consul.

1804
The Coronation

To prevent a royalist resurgence, Bonaparte asked the Senate to recreate the monarchy in his favour and to grant him the title of "Emperor of the French." In a plebiscite, the people confirmed this title and the hereditary nature of the new regime: Emperor Napoleon's descendants would inherit his powers.

To affirm his legitimacy in relation to the exiled heirs of the deceased Louis XVI and to outdo the traditional pageantry of kings, Napoleon decided to be crowned in the capital. Seeking to emulate Emperor Charlemagne, who had been crowned and anointed by the pope, he insisted that Pius VII attend his coronation.

However, he imposed a ritual that clearly affirmed his independence from the Church. Moreover, the event was held in Paris, rather than Rome. On December 2, in Notre-Dame Cathedral, Napoleon crowned himself, and the pope had to be content with offering his blessing.

Napoleon's Coronation Procession

1804–1805
Jacques Bertaux, oil on canvas

This painting shows the imperial procession on the morning of the coronation — December 2, 1804 — crossing the Pont-Neuf and turning left toward Notre-Dame Cathedral.

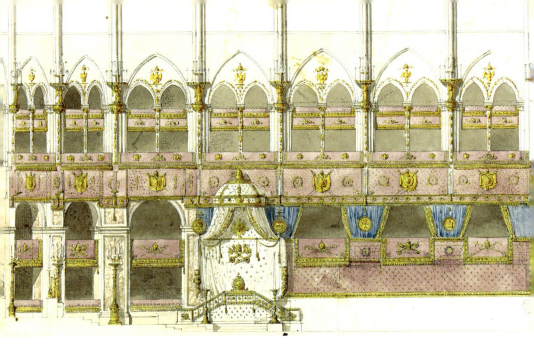

Decoration of Notre-Dame for Napoleon's Coronation (detail)

1804
Charles Percier, watercolour and wash

Architect Pierre Fontaine and his associate Charles Percier played an important role in the staging of the coronation ceremony, especially with respect to the decor. The Gothic style of Notre-Dame Cathedral was partially camouflaged for the occasion, both inside and out. This drawing shows plaques that feature Napoleon's great coat of arms.

Napoleon's Great Coat of Arms

1804
Gilded wood

This wall plaque was used to decorate Notre-Dame Cathedral for the coronation. Seeking to outdo the symbolism of the former monarchy, Napoleon revived heraldry. He adopted a great coat of arms featuring an eagle surrounded by a mantle strewn with bees.

Departure and Return from Military Campaigns

In the years following the coronation, war broke out again, and Napoleon found himself more often on military campaigns than in Paris. Preoccupied by war, he spent barely the equivalent of three years in the city between 1805 and 1814. Parisians celebrated the military achievements of their emperor and the Grande Armée. The Imperial Guard's entry into the city was always marked by great pomp.

Napoleon went easy on Paris, demanding fewer conscripts from the capital than the national average. Like the rest of the population, however, Parisians were still required to contribute to a never-ending war effort.

Napoleon's Camp Bed

1804–1815
Marie-Jean Desouches, iron and copper, re-created bedding

Practical furniture that was easy to dismantle and transport accompanied Napoleon whenever he left the capital. The Emperor was particularly delighted with this folding iron bed, created for him by Desouches, a Parisian locksmith.

The Conscripts of 1807 Marching Past Saint-Denis Gate

1808
Louis-Léopold Boilly
Oil on canvas

This painting illustrates the restrained enthusiasm shown by young men leaving for the army, as the population started to become aware of the massacres on the battlefields. The dark days of the Empire, when conscription would come to be seen as a calamity, were, however, still in the distant future.

1810
Marriage to Marie-Louise

In the spring of 1810, there were celebrations in Paris. Marie-Louise, the young Austrian archduchess, married Emperor Napoleon I, who had been divorced from Josephine de Beauharnais for less than six months. The civil wedding ceremony was held at the Saint-Cloud Palace, near Paris, on April 1. The religious ceremony followed the next day at the Tuileries.

Napoleon's objective was to found a dynasty and seal an alliance. He wanted Marie-Louise to give him the son that Josephine had been unable to give him. By marrying the eldest daughter of the emperor of Austria, he also sought to establish a special relationship with that major power, a long-time enemy of France.

Parisians were not very fond of Marie-Louise. She reminded them of Queen Marie-Antoinette, who was also Austrian, and whose frivolity and love of luxury had helped spark the French Revolution. The lavish wedding festivities, however, were a popular success. The people seemed to be more attached to the Emperor than ever.

Invitation Card, Emperor Napoleon's Wedding Ceremony

1810
Paper

Ceremonial for the Drafting of the Birth Certificate of the King of Rome

1811
Coloured etching

1811
The Birth of the King of Rome

Referring to his marriage to Marie-Louise, Napoleon crudely declared, "I'm marrying a womb." A year after the wedding, that womb gave him the long-awaited heir.

On March 20, 1811, at ten in the morning, cannon fire was heard throughout the capital. Parisians knew that the Empress was in the throes of labour and anxiously awaited news. The twenty-second salvo provoked shouts of joy: 21 guns were to be fired to celebrate the birth of a girl, and 101 for that of a boy. Napoléon François Charles Joseph Bonaparte had just been born after a difficult delivery. The child was given the title of King of Rome, a city that had been integrated into the French Empire two years earlier. The imperial dynasty was now assured. The prints published at the time to mark the event reflect the Emperor's joy tinged with pride. When he presented his son to the crowd, he apparently exclaimed, "The future belongs to me!"

1812
General Malet's Conspiracy

In 1812, Napoleon launched a military campaign against Russia that soon proved to be disastrous. Taking advantage of his absence from the capital, five generals attempted a *coup d'état*, led by General Claude François de Malet.

On October 23, the conspirators published a proclamation in Paris announcing the Emperor's death in Russia and the establishment of a provisional government: "Citizens, Bonaparte is no more! The avengers of humanity have dealt a blow to the tyrant.... Let us work together on public regeneration, let us become imbued with this great endeavour … which, in the eyes of Europe, will cleanse the nation of the infamies committed by the tyrant."

The plot hatched by Malet and his accomplices failed because of General Hulin, the military governor of Paris, who resisted them and had them arrested. Malet and thirteen other men were promptly court-martialled and condemned to death. They were shot on October 29.

When Napoleon learned of the events, he flew into one of his most formidable rages: Although he was presumed dead, no one had thought of proclaiming his son emperor in his place.

Execution of Generals Malet, Guidal, Lahorie and Company

1812
Jean Duplessis-Bertaux
Pen and ink on beige paper

***The Allied Prisoners of War Passing
Through Paris, Escorted by the National Guard,
February 17, 1814***

1814
Pierre-Michel Alix, watercoloured etching

1814
The Battle of Paris

After France's defeats in 1812 and 1813, the coalition formed by Russia, Prussia, Austria and Great Britain undertook its French Campaign in 1814. The French army won a few victories at Champaubert and Montmirail, east of the capital, but they were not enough.

At the end of March, the coalition forces — about 115,000 men — converged on Paris. While Napoleon and most of his army were held up far from the capital, the city was defended by only 40,000 men under the command of his brother Joseph. Parisian labourers and artisans were ready to fight to defend the capital.

They loudly demanded weapons, which the administration obstinately refused to provide, fearing an uprising against the regime.

At dawn on March 30, 1814, the members of the coalition launched a general attack. The day before, Joseph had encouraged Parisians to defend themselves by declaring, "I will stay with you," but he fled to Rambouillet, west of Paris, where Marie-Louise and the King of Rome had taken refuge. The fighting was extremely violent. On March 31, Paris fell.

1814–1815
The First Restoration

Before 1814, Paris had never endured foreign occupation. The French were shocked to see enemy troops entering the capital.

Napoleon signed his abdication at the Château de Fontainebleau, south of Paris, on April 6, and the monarchy was restored. Louis XVIII, born Louis Stanislas Xavier of France, Comte de Provence and heir of the king guillotined two decades earlier, arrived in Paris on May 3, having spent 23 years in exile.

The foreign occupation of Paris in 1814 and 1815 was peaceful. By order of Tsar Alexander I, the soldiers avoided committing acts of violence. As suggested by the print on page 45 — depicting a Russian officer saying goodbye to a Parisian woman — relations between the conquerors and the conquered could be cordial.

This first Restoration of the monarchy was short-lived. The endless missteps of the king and his entourage gave rise to nostalgia for the Empire, particularly among Parisians.

A Russian Saying Goodbye to a Parisian Woman

1814–1815
Philibert-Louis Debucourt,
after Carle Vernet
Colour aquatint

The One France Longs For

Around 1814–1815
Oil on canvas mounted on cardboard

This work reflects what many people in France thought of Louis XVIII during the first Restoration. Behind the profile of the new king, who was overweight and suffered from gout, there is a hidden image of Napoleon.

LE DESIRE DE LA FRANCE

1815
The Hundred Days

On March 20, 1815, Napoleon arrived in the capital. He had escaped from the island of Elba, in the Mediterranean, where the major powers had exiled him. The news of his return stunned everyone. He was well received by Parisians, especially the working class and the army.

Russia, Austria, Prussia and Great Britain, whose representatives were meeting at the Congress of Vienna, directed their armies against Napoleon once again. His defeat at Waterloo on June 18 put an end to this final epic, which has become known as the "Hundred Days."

On June 22, 1815, back in the capital, Napoleon admitted defeat. He took refuge in the Élysée Bourbon Palace. There, despite the pleas of the Parisians who came to cheer him, he signed his act of abdication. Realizing that his political life was over, he proclaimed his son, Napoleon II, Emperor of the French. But the major powers rejected the succession and placed Louis XVIII back on the throne, inaugurating the second Restoration.

"We have destroyed everything. We must now rebuild. There is a government. There are powers. But what about the rest of the nation? What is it? Grains of sand.... We are scattered, without a system, lacking unity and contact. As long as I am here, I will certainly answer for the republic, but we must look ahead. Do you think that the republic is well established? If so, you are greatly mistaken. We are free to make it so, but we have not, and we will not unless we cast some masses of granite upon the soil of France."

— *Napoleon*

Collar of a Grand Master of the Order of the Legion of Honour, Owned by Napoleon

Around 1807
Martin-Guillaume Biennais
Silver, gold, enamel

THE ADMINISTRATION OF THE CITY

Organizing the Capital

With the law of 28 Pluviôse, Year VIII (February 17, 1800), promulgated shortly after the *coup d'état* that gave him power, Napoleon Bonaparte reorganized the country and its capital. He did his best to gain exclusive control of Paris.

Napoleon withdrew authority from elected representatives, handing it instead to administrators, police officers and engineers, all of whom were directly beholden to him. During the Revolution, Paris had been divided into twelve *arrondissements*. That did not change. However, the position of mayor of Paris was abolished.

Each *arrondissement* retained its own mayor, but henceforth they would be appointed by the State. In charge of civil registration and information, they were essentially intermediaries between the administration and those it governed.

The Administrative Council was the entity that made the real decisions concerning Paris. Chaired by Napoleon himself, its meetings were usually attended by the Minister of the Interior, the presidents of the Interior and War sections of the State Council, the Minister of Police, the Minister of Public Works, the prefect.

of the Seine, the prefect of police and, often, engineers and architects.

The position of prefect was established by the law of 28 Pluviôse, Year VIII. In Paris, the prefect of the Seine was responsible for general administration related to civil registration, religion, elections, conscription, hospices and asylums, prisons, public education, public works, and direct and indirect taxes. He presided over the Prefecture Council, which examined contentious matters related to public administration and taxes. He worked closely with the prefect of police, who was responsible for maintaining order and for related matters: residency permits, vagrancy, imprisonment, surveillance and censorship, roads, public hygiene, fires and floods.

The General Council, composed of 24 members, served as a municipal council and met at city hall. Although it was responsible for approving the budget, it merely rubber-stamped the decisions made by the prefects.

The Minister of Public Works was responsible for the construction and maintenance of the capital's infrastructure.

Jean-Antoine Chaptal

Year VIII (1799–1800)
Louis-André-Gabriel Bouchet
Oil on canvas

A renowned industrialist and chemist, Chaptal served as Minister of the Interior from 1800 to 1804. On behalf of Bonaparte, he drafted the law of 28 Pluviôse, Year VIII (February 17, 1800), which gave Paris the centralized organization it maintained for nearly two centuries.

Masses of Granite

Napoleon used the expression "masses of granite" when referring to the new institutions aimed at restoring social cohesion in the capital and the country as a whole after ten years of revolution.

In addition to creating the position of prefect (1800), Napoleon founded the Bank of France (1800), standardized the franc (1803) and encouraged industry. He paid particular attention to legal reforms, publishing the Civil Code (1804), the Code of Civil Procedure (1806), the Code of Commerce (1807) and the Penal Code (1810).

To reward outstanding military and civil achievements, and win over the notables, Napoleon created the national order of the Legion of Honour (1802). He is said to have once stated, "It is with such baubles that men are led."

In 1802, Napoleon established *lycées* (high schools), a new type of institution for secondary education. He also took an interest in the Musée du Louvre, where the national collections had been housed since 1792. In 1802, it became the Musée Napoléon.

Religious freedom, prohibited during the Revolution, had been re-established in 1795. Catholicism was no longer the State religion, but it remained the faith of a majority of the population. The Concordat (1801) placed it under the protection and supervision of the State. Religious services thus resumed in churches that had stood empty.

Napoleon also introduced a degree of religious pluralism, officially recognizing the Protestant (1802) and Jewish (1808) communities.

Bust of Napoleon I

1805
Lorenzo Bartolini, François Rémond and François Damerart
Bronze

In the days of the Empire, this massive bust was set in a niche above the main entrance of the Musée Napoléon. The neck is elongated because this depiction of the Emperor in Roman attire was to be viewed from below.

Joseph Fouché,
Duke of Otranto

1815
Engraving, stippling, bistre

Police and Public Opinion

Napoleon placed public spaces under heavy surveillance. Having assumed power following a decade of political instability, he knew that it was in the capital that regimes were made and unmade.

Joseph Fouché was Minister of the General Police from 1799 to 1802 and from 1804 to 1810. With the help of his network of agents, he doggedly pursued conspirators and those who criticized the Consulate and the Empire. Referring to him, Napoleon wrote: "Intrigue was as necessary to Fouché as food; he intrigued all the time, everywhere, in every way and with everyone."

The police controlled access to the city, monitoring arrivals and departures at its gates. The prisons were also under their responsibility. Informers, dubbed *mouches* (flies), walked the streets, and frequented public gardens, cafés and other places where people went to enjoy themselves. The police monitored all celebrations and establishments that were open to the public: theatres, dance halls, gambling houses, brothels, swim clubs and public baths. Their objective was to ensure good moral conduct and to maintain order while sounding public opinion and uncovering political intrigue. Each day, the First Consul — then the Emperor — received bulletins informing him of the mood in the capital.

The Passage des Panoramas, Théâtre des Variétés

Around 1800–1805
Anonymous
Gouache

As the Directory came to an end, covered passages became a feature of the capital's landscape. In these lively places, all the enticing material goods made possible by the regime's prosperity were on display.

The Galleries of the Palais-Royal

1809
Louis-Léopold Boillym, oil on canvas

The gardens, galleries and theatres of the Palais-Royal, north of the Louvre Palace, were a fashionable meeting place. An observer wrote at the time, "Paris is the capital of France, and the Palais-Royal is the capital of Paris." In the evening, prostitutes sold their charms there. It is said that, when he was a young second lieutenant, Bonaparte himself lost his virginity there in 1787.

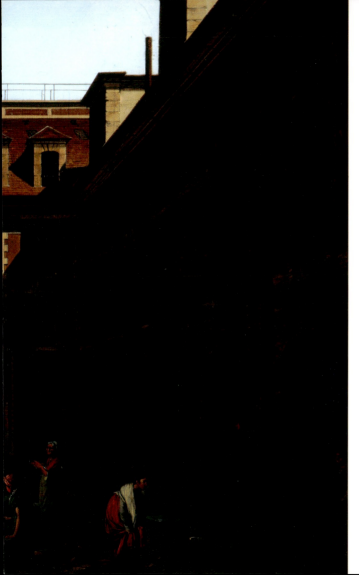

Madelonnettes Prison

Around 1810
Louis-Léopold Boilly
Oil on canvas

The prefect of police oversaw Paris's prisons. He was responsible for placing prisoners in jail, arranging transfers and releases, and allowing or forbidding visits. The former Madelonnettes Convent housed women who were charged, detained and sentenced to less than five years in prison.

Armchair from the Emperor's State Cabinet at the Tuileries

1814
François-Honoré-Georges Jacob-Desmalter
Gilded wood, leather, velvet, embroidery

The Cabinet and the Administrative Council met in the state cabinet at the Tuileries Palace. Everyone sat around a round table, but only the Emperor had an armchair. This swivel armchair was delivered in 1814.

THE COURT AT THE TUILERIES

"Power and pageantry go hand in hand. I had to project an image, to appear grave, to establish rules of etiquette. Otherwise, people would have slapped me on the shoulder daily."

— *Napoleon*

The Tuileries Palace

In 1800, First Consul Bonaparte moved into the Tuileries. Built in the centre of Paris during the Renaissance, where a tile (*tuile* in French) factory had once stood, this former royal palace had been the last official residence of Louis XVI. Since it was damaged during the Revolution, major renovations were undertaken in the fifteen years that Napoleon was in power. Little by little, it was decorated and furnished, and court life re re-emerged there.

The second floor of the west wing housed the Emperor's private apartments, as well as the state apartments, where the throne room and the state cabinet were located. The Empress's apartments were on the ground floor.

Architects Percier and Fontaine transformed the former kings' state chamber into a throne room for Napoleon's coronation. It became the most important room in the palace when it came to protocol. In addition to being a site of pomp and circumstance, the Tuileries Palace was a place of incessant work. The Cabinet and the Administrative Council both met in the state cabinet.

The gardens are all that remains of the Tuileries Palace, which was burned down in 1871 during the Commune insurrection.

The Tuileries Gardens and Palace Seen from the Quai d'Orsay

1813
Étienne Bouhot, oil on canvas

The Sovereigns Together at the Ball Given by the City of Paris

1809
Adrien-Pierre-François Godefroy, coloured etching

On December 4, 1809, the City of Paris gave a reception to celebrate the peace treaty with Austria and the fifth anniversary of Napoleon's coronation. Napoleon is shown here surrounded by friends and relatives. From left to right: Joachim Murat, King of Naples and the Emperor's brother-in-law; Frederick Augustus, King of Saxony; Jerome, King of Westphalia; Frederick, King of Wurtemberg; Louis, King of Holland; Napoleon and Josephine; Napoleon's mother; Julie, Queen of Spain; Hortense, Queen of Holland; Caroline, Queen of Naples; Catherine, Queen of Westphalia; and Pauline, Princess Borghese.

The Imperial Family

The imperial court's inner circle consisted of Napoleon's family, which was divided into two rival groups. On one side, there were the Bonapartes: Napoleon's mother, brothers (Joseph, Lucien, Louis and Jerome) and sisters (Pauline, Élisa and Caroline). On the other, the Beauharnais: his wife, Josephine; his stepson, Eugene; and his stepdaughter, Hortense. Josephine's in-laws detested her, but the public liked her because she was friendly and kind.

Marie-Louise, who succeeded Josephine in 1810, put much more distance between herself and the public, but she turned out to be an ideal second wife for Napoleon. A princess of the House of Austria, she had been raised to be obedient. She was devoted and affectionate toward her new husband. Much to the surprise of courtiers, she addressed him informally, calling him Nana or Popo.

Because Napoleon was busy fighting wars in Russia, Germany and France, he spent little time with his son, Napoléon François Charles Joseph Bonaparte, the King of Rome, nicknamed l'Aiglon (the Eaglet). When he first went into exile, in 1814, Marie-Louise took the child to Vienna. He died there in 1832, at the young age of 21.

Dignitaries and Courtiers

The princes and princesses of the imperial family, dignitaries, and figures who held high civilian or military positions formed the core of the imperial court. A host of officers and senior public servants revolved around them.

Napoleon, who knew that appearances mattered, was particularly attentive to the design of the uniforms he wanted to see around him. Official dress for public servants was established by decree. The colours, embroidery and materials indicated a person's rank within the hierarchy. Preferring work, however, to the formality of court life, Napoleon often became rude and impatient during lengthy court ceremonies.

Although the French Revolution had raised hopes of equality between the sexes, the Empire period proved to be a difficult time for women. The Civil Code that Napoleon introduced in 1804 granted them no political or civil rights. Women were to be, above all, wives and mothers. At court, their function was ornamental. The wives of dignitaries and important officials did their best to imitate the women of the imperial family in every way.

Talleyrand

1807
Pierre-Paul Prud'hon
Oil on canvas

Napoleon's Minister of Foreign Affairs, Charles-Maurice de Talleyrand-Périgord, was one of the most influential figures of the time. Here, he wears the official dress of the Grand Chamberlain, an office he held from 1804 to 1809. When he fell from grace for actions Napoleon considered treasonous, the Emperor apparently told him, "You are filth in a silk stocking."

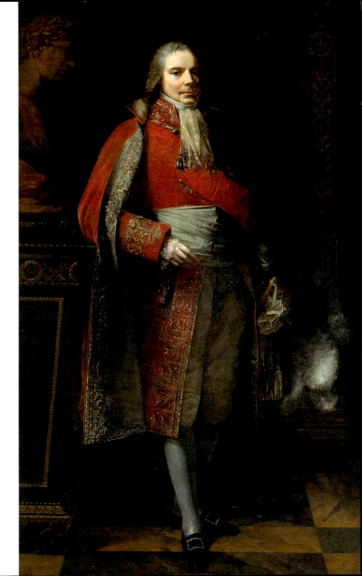

Chamberlain's Keys

After 1804, gilded bronze

The chamberlains' symbol of office was a gilded key worn at waist level. These important civilian officers were assigned to the bedchambers of the Emperor, the Empress and the sovereigns of the imperial family, and coordinated any services required. Often drawn from families of the former nobility who supported the new regime, they were among the most influential figures at court.

Gaudin, Duke of Gaeta

1806
Joseph-Marie Vien, known as Vien the Younger
Oil on canvas

Martin-Michel-Charles Gaudin, Duke of Gaeta, was Minister of Finance from 1800 to 1815. Since Napoleon trusted him, he worked closely with him. In this portrait, he is shown in official ministerial dress and leans on his portfolio, the ultimate symbol of Napoleonic government.

Official Suppliers to the Court

The luxury-goods industry, which had made Paris one of the great European centres for craftspeople, had suffered during the Revolution because much of its clientele had emigrated. Under the Consulate and the Empire, however, new official orders revived production.

Napoleon had 47 palaces at his disposal, most of which the revolutionaries had emptied. The renewed pomp associated with his regime called for new, prestigious surroundings and objects symbolizing the nation's grandeur. The work of the cabinetmakers, goldsmiths, silversmiths, jewellers, porcelain makers, bronzesmiths and tailors who were official suppliers to the court gave birth to the Empire style.

By reviving the pageantry of the monarchy, Napoleon sought to put some distance between himself and his subjects. His luxurious way of life satisfied his taste for comfort, his desire for order and his politics of splendour.

Shopfronts and Decors

1806–1828
Pierre de La Mésengère, watercoloured etchings

At the time, engravings of the façades of fashionable boutiques were produced to serve as inspiration for other establishments. Several of those merchants were official suppliers to the imperial court. Jeweller Marie-Étienne Nitot and his son, for example, created the splendid jewellery for Napoleon's weddings to Josephine and Marie-Louise.

Campaign Kit of Napoleon I

Around 1805, Martin-Guillaume Biennais, mahogany, brass, Morocco leather, gilded silver, silver, crystal, porcelain, tortoiseshell, ebony, ivory, steel

Both simple and ingenious, this kit illustrates the skill of the suppliers to the imperial court. It contains about 110 items: work instruments, tableware and grooming accessories. Napoleon ordered many kits from Biennais, a goldsmith, but this one was his favourite. He took it with him to the battles of Ulm, Austerlitz, Jena, Eylau and Friedland.

Furniture of the Duke and Duchess of Gaeta

1800–1820

This furniture was acquired between 1800 and 1820 by Martin-Michel-Charles Gaudin, Duke of Gaeta, Napoleon's Minister of Finance, and by his wife, Anna Sommaripa. Made of mahogany or mahogany veneer and enhanced with gilded bronze ornamentation, it reflects the tastes of the new elites. It is a good example of the Empire style, characterized by motifs inspired by ancient Rome. Its massive forms, right angles and lack of mouldings distinguish it from the furniture of the previous century, which tended to be lighter.

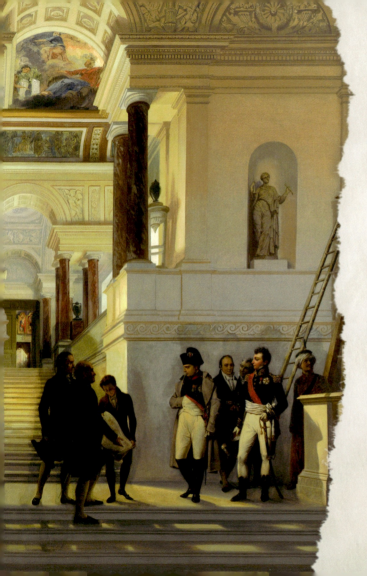

Napoleon I Viewing the Staircase of the Louvre, Accompanied by Architects Percier and Fontaine

1833
Louis-Charles-Auguste Couder
Oil on canvas

THE CITY OF HIS DREAMS

"Paris is superior to France's other cities. I wanted this capital to be so splendid that it would dwarf all the capitals in the universe. I did everything, and wanted to do everything, for Paris."

— *Napoleon*

The Parisian Landscape After the Revolution

When Napoleon Bonaparte took power, Paris looked more or less the same as it had under Louis XVI. The revolutionary authorities had begun work on ambitious projects, but they were not able to transform the capital for lack of time.

During the Revolution, properties belonging to the nobility and the clergy were confiscated and sold as national assets. In the days of the Consulate and the Empire, real-estate speculation and urban planning led to the destruction or repurposing of several churches, convents and mansions.

Paris still resembled a medieval city in many respects. Its public gardens were well maintained, but its streets were narrow and winding, and in a pitiful state. They became rivers of mud when it rained, and it was not uncommon to see people relieving themselves anywhere they liked. There were no covered markets or slaughterhouses, so the streets were filled with merchants, and animals were butchered there. Fountains were rare and often dry.

The Church of the Feuillants Being Demolished

Around 1804
Hubert Robert
Oil on canvas

Percier and Fontaine: The Major Projects Team

The Parisian architectural community boasted the refined talent and expertise needed to serve a sovereign. From this community, Napoleon chose his principal architects. Pierre Fontaine and Charles Percier, former classmates at the Académie royale d'architecture in Paris and the Académie de France in Rome, entered the First Consul's service in January 1801.

Fontaine was named First Architect by Napoleon. He was the one who dealt with their prestigious patron and managed the many projects entrusted to him and his partner. Percier preferred to devote himself to producing drawings in the privacy of his office. The work of this prolific duo, which characterized the Empire style, ranged from interior decoration to the urban restructuring of entire neighbourhoods. They remained the Emperor's favourites until the very end.

Monuments

Seeking to beautify the capital and leave a physical reminder of the grandeur of his reign, Napoleon endowed Paris with prestigious buildings.

He decided to fill the capital with monuments largely inspired by those of antiquity. Architects already had a preference for the neoclassical style, which draws upon Greco-Roman forms, but it became more pronounced in the days of the Empire. Ancient Rome, in particular, offered an example of power and permanence. Multiple arches, columns and temples were erected in Paris, recording in stone the glory of France's armies.

Napoleon also had the Tuileries Palace renovated and the surrounding area redeveloped, transforming the site from which he exercised power.

The Arc de Triomphe du Carrousel

1808–1815
Louis-Pierre Baltard
Sepia wash

Napoleon is said to have told his soldiers at Austerlitz, "You will return to your homes only through arches of triumph." In ancient Rome, such monumental arches commemorated military victories. In 1806, Napoleon ordered the construction of two arches, including the Arc de Triomphe du Carrousel across from the central pavilion of the Tuileries Palace.

The Étoile site, at the end of the Champs-Élysées, was chosen as the location of the second triumphal arch ordered by Napoleon. The first stone of the Arc de Triomphe de l'Étoile was laid in 1806, but when Napoleon and Marie-Louise were married, four years later, its construction was still in the early stages. A temporary structure, made of wood and canvas painted in *trompe l'œil*, was erected on its stone foundation to mark the entry of the imperial couple. It is said that Napoleon left Paris for the last time, in 1815, through the incomplete arch. The Arc de Triomphe de l'Étoile was not completed until 1836.

Design for the Completion of the Madeleine as a Temple of Glory

Around 1805
François-Jacques Delannoy, outline colour wash

The Madeleine Church, whose construction began in 1764, had not been completed. Napoleon considered turning it into a temple to the glory of the French armies. This drawing shows one of the projects submitted to the competition for completion.

House, Rue de Rivoli

1809
Jean-Charles Krafft,
after Charles Percier
and Pierre Fontaine
Etching and engraving

Dating back two centuries, the idea of joining the Tuileries and the Louvre, two royal residences, was revived at Napoleon's request. To beautify the neighbourhood around the two palaces, which were now imperial residences, and to streamline its organization, Napoleon requested the development of the Rue de Rivoli. The project was entrusted to Percier and Fontaine. The name of the street, which maintains its period character to this day, refers to one of the young General Bonaparte's most resounding victories, against the Austrians in Italy.

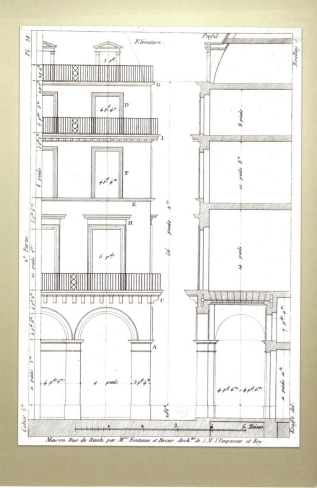

Utilitarian Structures

The new Napoleonic Paris was as much a city of amenities as a city of monuments. Often annoyed by his architects' expensive tastes, Napoleon was more at ease when it came to public works and functional buildings. The Emperor innovated by attaching as much importance to utilitarian facilities as to prestigious buildings.

Along with the new bridges that made it easy for Parisians to cross the Seine, the construction of the Ourcq Canal to supply water for Paris was one of the major achievements of Napoleon's engineers. Fountains, quays, markets and slaughterhouses were built throughout the city. The new structures were characterized by their simplicity: symmetrical floor plans and façades, basic geometry, distance from neighbouring buildings and minimal ornamentation.

In the days of the Consulate and the Empire, a concern for public health led to the creation of new cemeteries and the development of former underground quarries, which were converted into catacombs.

The Emperor Visiting the Wine and Spirits Warehouse

1811
Étienne Bouhot, oil on canvas

Interior View of the Catacombs

1816
James Forbes
Pen, India ink wash

Projects Left on the Drawing Board

In the fifteen years that he was in power, Napoleon initiated more projects than he could complete. In addition to the Arc de Triomphe de l'Étoile, he considered building public baths or an obelisk on the Pont-Neuf, and erecting a column in Place de la Concorde. Two other projects stand out.

In 1810, Napoleon ordered the construction of a fountain featuring an elephant in Place de la Bastille. The animal was to be cast in bronze from cannons seized from enemy armies and to bear a tower on its back, recalling the military use of elephants in antiquity. A full-sized plaster model was created in 1814 and stood on the site for some 30 years.

Afterwards, the foundation on which the elephant was to have been set became the base of the Colonne de Juillet (July Column), which still stands.

Napoleon's most ambitious project, however, was the massive residence conceived by Percier and Fontaine for the Emperor on Chaillot Hill, and the new neighbourhood to be built across from it. Starting in 1811, the planned building was referred to as the Palace of the King of Rome, in honour of Napoleon's soon-to-be-born son. The construction began in May, but when the Empire fell, that grandiose undertaking was abandoned.

Design for the Elephant Fountain, Place de la Bastille

1810–1815
Jean-Antoine Alavoine Le Chevalier
Outline watercolour

The Palace of the King of Rome, Viewed from the Main Road

Around 1810–1812
Pierre Fontaine
Pen and wash

Model of Napoleon's Tomb

After 1861
Marble, bronze,
felt, brass

THE LEGEND IN PARIS

"I want my remains to be laid to rest on the banks of the Seine, among the French people that I loved so dearly."

— *Napoleon*

From St. Helena to Les Invalides

Following Napoleon's fall in 1815 and his death in 1821, the image of the Emperor with the famous silhouette — the heir of the Revolution, the man of the people, the fellow soldier — was ardently kept alive, particularly by the men who had fought alongside him. The "Napoleonic legend" inspired an abundant iconography and numerous literary works. The human cost of the Napoleonic Wars was set aside in favour of a nostalgic effect emphasizing Napoleon's heroism and immortality.

In 1830, a new Parisian revolution forced the abdication of Charles X, who had succeeded his brother Louis XVIII. The new king, Louis-Philippe of Orléans, and his government took measures designed to revive the Napoleonic legend and gain the support of the Bonapartist party. In 1840, he had the Emperor's body moved from St. Helena to Paris.

The Hôtel des Invalides was chosen to house the Emperor's remains because of its close association with the military. It had been established under Louis XIV to serve as both a hospital and a hospice for disabled veterans, and Napoleon had devoted a lot of attention to it. After the fall of the Empire, the site had remained emblematic to Bonapartists.

The Remains of Napoleon I Being Taken Ashore at Courbevoie, December 15, 1840

1840
Victor Adam, oil on canvas

Scale Model of Napoleon's Coffin

1840
Louis-Édouard Lemarchand
Ebony, bronze

Napoleonic souvenirs abounded in the 19th century. This model is a replica of the coffin in which the Emperor's remains were transported from St. Helena to Paris, and was made with remnants of the ebony used to build the actual coffin.

The coffin carrying Napoleon's remains left St. Helena, in the South Atlantic, on October 8, 1840, and arrived at Cherbourg, France, on November 30. There, it was transferred to a steamboat and taken along the Seine to Courbevoie, eight kilometres upriver from Paris, reaching its destination on December 15. The funeral procession, followed by a massive crowd, then headed to Les Invalides, where it was met by the king himself. A lavish setting was created for the return of Napoleon's remains. The imperial eagle — a motif not seen since the Restoration — resurfaced.

In 1842, an extensive competition was held for the design of Napoleon's tomb, and Louis Visconti was selected as the architect. Napoleon's remains were finally laid to rest in the tomb in 1861.

Emperor Napoleon III

After 1852
Anonymous
Lithograph

Napoleon I in the Days of Napoleon III

Exiled after 1815, Louis-Napoleon Bonaparte became heir presumptive to the imperial throne following the death of his older brother and that of his cousin, the King of Rome. He was both a nephew of Napoleon I and a grandson of Empress Josephine, who was his maternal grandmother. Taking advantage of the French Revolution of 1848, he was elected president of the Republic. On December 2, 1851, he staged a *coup d'état* that allowed him to restore the Empire the following year. He was proclaimed emperor under the name Napoleon III.

Napoleon III constantly presented himself as his uncle's heir. This prestigious lineage became the foundation of the symbolic construction of his regime. The new emperor immediately brought back the emblems of earlier times: the *N*, the great coat of arms, the eagle, the bees, and the colours crimson and gold.

Napoleon III transformed Paris with the help of Prefect Georges-Eugène Haussmann. Most of the utilitarian structures built during the Consulate and the First Empire disappeared, but the names of the heroes and victories of the Napoleonic era were reintegrated into the urban landscape. The official cult of Napoleon I reached its height.

The defeat of France by Prussia in 1870 triggered the fall of Napoleon III.

Apotheosis of Napoleon I, Copy of the Sketch for the Ceiling of the Napoleon III Salon at Paris City Hall

Around 1870
Louise Tisserand, after Jean-Auguste-Dominique Ingres
Paint on porcelain

Napoleon III asked Ingres, who had produced some of the most striking portraits of Napoleon I, to paint a ceiling at Paris City Hall in honour of his predecessor. The artist depicted the Emperor being elevated to the rank of a god in Greco-Roman fashion. The work was destroyed in a fire in 1871, during the Commune uprising.

The Trials and Tribulations of the Vendôme Column

The most emblematic monument of the Napoleonic legend in Paris is the Vendôme Column, located in the middle of Place Vendôme. As regimes and revolutions came and went, three statues succeeded one another atop the column.

In 1803, First Consul Bonaparte decided to erect a column similar to the one honouring the emperor Trajan in Rome. Built between 1806 and 1810, it was dedicated to the Grande Armée and surmounted by a statue of Napoleon as a Roman emperor. In 1814, the statue was melted down by order of King Louis XVIII.

In 1833, King Louis-Philippe placed a new statue of Napoleon on top of the Vendôme Column. Sculptor Charles Émile Seurre depicted the Emperor as the Little Corporal, wearing his frock coat and his bicorne. In 1863, Napoleon III had that statue replaced by one portraying his uncle as a Roman emperor once again.

In 1871, in the wake of France's defeat by Prussia, the Paris Commune had the column knocked down, viewing it as a "monument to barbarism, and a symbol of brute force and false glory." Less than a week later, the National Assembly decided to erect it once again. The reconstruction began in 1873 and was completed in 1875. Napoleon regained his place atop the column, as a Roman emperor.

Model of the Vendôme Column

Around 1833–1864
Bronze with a marble base

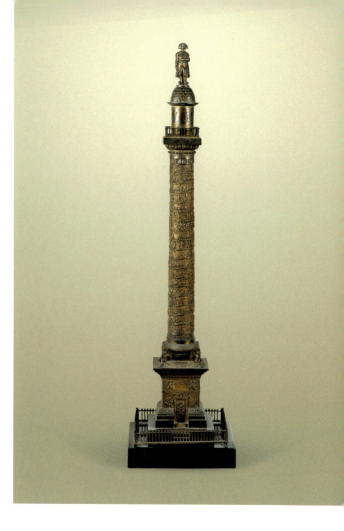

A group next to the debris of the Vendôme Column during the Commune

1871
Attributed to
Auguste-Bruno Braquehais

"Despite all the attempts made to belittle me, get rid of me or reduce me to silence, it will be difficult to make me disappear completely from public memory."

— *Napoleon*

Napoleon's Bicorne

Around 1810
Beaver felt, silk cockade

In an era when a general's bicorne was usually covered with braiding and feathers, Napoleon opted for a model with no hint of luxury. He also wore his hat *en bataille* (sideways), whereas most officers wore theirs *en colonne* (perpendicular to the body). The Emperor had eight bicornes delivered to him each year by the Parisian hatmaker Poupard. He wore this one in 1810.

Contributions

The **Napoleon and Paris** exhibition was produced by the Musée Carnavalet – Histoire de Paris, Paris Musées and the Canadian Museum of History. Its texts were adapted from those written by Thierry Sarmant, Florian Meunier, Charlotte Duvette and Philippe de Carbonnières for the original exhibition, **Napoléon et Paris – Rêves d'une capitale** (Napoleon and Paris — Dreams of a Capital), presented at the Musée Carnavalet in 2015, and the accompanying catalogue (*Napoléon et Paris – Rêves d'une capitale*, Musée Carnavalet and Paris Musées, 2015).

We would like to express our sincere gratitude to the institutions and collectors who contributed to the Canadian adaptation of this exhibition. In alphabetical order: the Bank of France, Bruno Ledoux and the Société LUPB, the Château de Fontainebleau, the Desmarais Trust, the Fondation Napoléon, the Maritime Museum of the Atlantic, the Mobilier national, the Musée de l'Armée, the Musée du Louvre, the Musée national des châteaux de Malmaison et Bois Préau, and the Palais Galliera.

The Canadian Museum of History is greatly indebted to the following members of its staff for their commitment to this project: Sophie Doucet, Project Manager; Jean-François Léger, Creative Development Specialist; and Chantal Baril, Scenographer. Several other colleagues, including Erin Gurski, April Tessier, Stéphane Breton, Mélissa Duncan and Louis Lebel, assisted greatly. Frédéric St-Laurent and Michel Paquette, of Visou Design, also made an invaluable contribution by designing the exhibition. We also thank Line Majeau, Sheila Singhal, Paula Sousa, Josée Malenfant, Diane Hardy and Lee Wyndham for their role in the editing, translation and revision of the texts.

Photo Credits

© **Canadian Museum of History / Steven Darby**
p. 6

© **Musée Carnavalet / Roger-Viollet**
p. 8, 18, 22, 25, 26, 29, 30, 34, 37, 38, 41, 42, 45, 46, 53, 56, 58, 59, 60, 65, 67, 71, 73, 74, 79, 82, 84, 85, 87, 88, 90, 92, 97, 100

Bruno Ledoux Collection
p. 12, 21, 31

© **Stéphane Piera / Musée Carnavalet / Roger Viollet**
p. 15, 69, 75, 98

© **Coll. particulière, Montréal**
p. 17, 109

Mobilier National Collection © **Isabelle Bideau**
p. 33

© **Musée de l'Armée / Dist. RMN-Grand Palais / Art Resource, NY**
p. 50

© **RMN-Grand Palais / Art Resource, NY**
p. 55, 62

© **Fondation Napoléon / Patrice Maurin Berthier**
p. 70

© **Musée du Louvre, Dist. RMN-Grand Palais / Martine Beck-Coppola / Art Resource, NY**
p. 76

© **Fondation Napoléon / Thomas Hennocque**
p. 94

© **Petit Palais / Roger-Viollet**
p. 102

© **Eric Emo / Musée Carnavalet / Roger-Viollet**
p. 105

© **Bruno Braquehais / BHVP / Roger-Viollet**
p. 106

© **Studio Sébert – photographes**
p. 109